OCEAN WILDLIFE

GALLERY BOOKS

An Imprint of W. H. Smith Publishers Inc.

112 Madison Avenue
New York City 10016

This edition first published in U.S.
in 1990 by Gallery Books,
an imprint of W.H. Smith Publishers, Inc.
112 Madison Avenue, New York, New York 10016

ISBN 0-8317-9585-9

Printed and bound in Spain

For rights information about the photographs in
this book please contact:

The Image Bank
111 Fifth Avenue, New York, N.Y. 10003

Producer: Solomon M. Skolnick
Author: Lynda DeWitt
Design Concept: Leslie Ehlers
Designer: Ann-Louise Lipman
Editor: Madelyn Larsen
Production: Valerie Zars
Photo Researcher: Edward Douglas
Assistant Photo Researcher: Robert Hale

Title page: **Close-up of the mantle of a giant clam.** *Opposite:* **A butterfly fish cruises among soft coral in the Red Sea. Butterfly fish live worldwide in warm waters. Their multicolored patterns camouflage their eyes, making it difficult for predators to know if they are coming or going.**

Imagine yourself on a camping trip in the wilderness. Your tent rests not on a mountain ridge or in a patch of woods, but on the ocean floor, ten stories below the surface of the water. You won't need boots or backpacks here. To explore your surroundings, you wear a pressurized suit and carry your own oxygen. You're not indoors, but you're not exactly outdoors either. Look up, and you can't see the moon or the stars.

Today, people studying the ocean may spend weeks at a time underwater. Swimming by day and returning to their tent, or "underwater habitat," to eat, sleep, and record notes, they search for answers to such basic questions as where do fish spawn and how do the waters of the oceans move. A myriad of high-tech tools – satellites, acoustic CAT scanners, and remote-controlled subs – are helping them unlock these and other secrets of the sea. Until recently, less was known about the ocean floor than the surface of the moon.

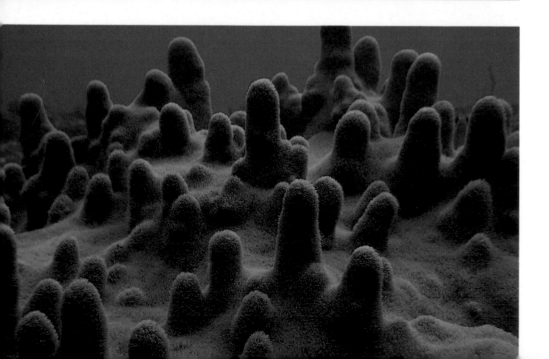

Top to bottom: **Another sedentary animal, the crinoid, or feather star, traps animal larvae and other floating food particles with its branching appendages. The limestone skeleton of soft coral lies inside transparent branches. Shielded by the coral, a small grouper waits in ambush. A colony of pillar coral off Puerto Rico's coast looks like a cactus garden on some dry, alien planet. Coral consists of cylindrical animals, called polyps, encased in immobile limestone skeletons. Algae living on the polyps provide them with oxygen and nutrients.**

A velvet starfish, or sea star, creeps along the ocean floor off the coast of Mexico. The animal inches forward on tiny tube feet—appendages with suction discs—lining the underside of each arm. The starfish uses its tube feet to pry open the shells of oysters and scallops. *Right:* A plume worm off California's coast extracts food and oxygen from the water.

Sea squirts, or sea grapes, are bottom-dwellers that use their gills to filter food from seawater. *Left:* Sharp spines on these starfish help ward off enemies. Still, predators able to flip them over can feed on their soft underbelly. A crown-of-thorns starfish, in the foreground, feeds on coral polyps. *Opposite:* Flowerlike tentacles, surrounding the mouths of sea anemones, can inject a paralyzing poison into prey. Sea anemones are polyps that remain fixed to the ocean floor, a rock, or the shell of a crab or some other animal.

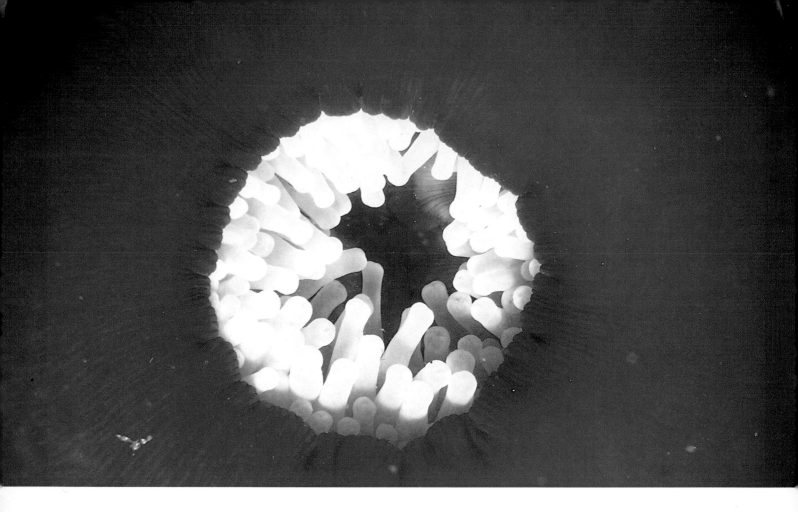

Tentacles of a sea anemone open and close as they gather food. When disturbed, the anemone pulls in its tentacles and shortens its body. *Below:* Clownfish live in the arms of sea anemones. Slimy secretions on their bodies protect them from the stinging tentacles. In exchange for a safe hiding place the brightly colored clownfish lure other fishes within the anemones' grasp.

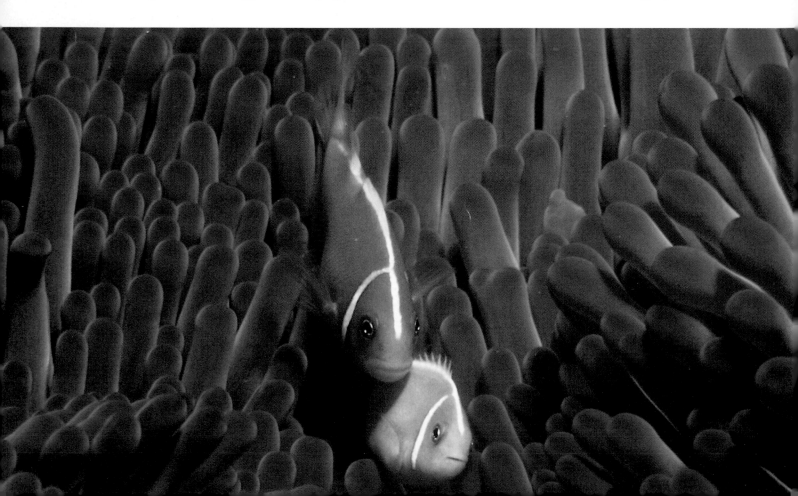

Yet the oceans – actually, one huge interlocking sea – cover more than 70 percent of the earth's surface. With "borders" in place, the Pacific ranks as the largest, followed by the Atlantic, Indian, and the ice-covered Arctic. The waters surrounding the continent of Antarctica are generally considered the southern reaches of the Pacific, Atlantic, and Indian oceans, rather than a separate ocean.

Like the air above them, the oceans stay in constant motion. Pulled by the gravity of the moon, ocean waters rise and fall twice daily, creating tides. Waves bulge across the surface from shoreline to shoreline. They may appear as gently rising ripples one day and as speeding mountains of water the next. Affecting only an ocean's top layer, tides and waves move water vertically.

Currents, each carrying water of similar temperature and density, flow horizontally from the top to the bottom of the oceans. As warm waters of the tropics expand northward, cold polar waters sink and flow south. Shaped by the gravity and rotation of the earth, large circular currents, or gyres, spin in each of the oceans.

The foot-long (30 cm) garibaldi lives within kelp forests off rocky, cold-water coasts. This bold and bright fish will steal food from larger animals and chase intruders from its territory. *Below:* Soldier fish dwell along reefs or rocks in tropical waters. Large eyes enable them to hunt at night.

Blue-striped snappers swim off the Maldive Islands in the Indian Ocean. These colorful members of the grunt family usually travel in schools.

Top to bottom: **A coral reef in the Red Sea is home to this Picasso triggerfish. A blue-girdled angelfish finds refuge in warm shallow waters off Papua New Guinea. A French angelfish looks for sponges and sea squirts off the Cayman Islands in the Caribbean Sea. French angelfish range in waters from Florida to Brazil.**

Churning within this brew are the ingredients of life; most of the elements on earth, including calcium, cobalt, iron, magnesium, silver, sulfur, and zinc, are found dissolved in seawater. In fact, the same proportion of elements found in seawater exists within our bodies.

Animals of the sea rely on plants for survival. Like their terrestrial counterparts, aquatic plants undergo photosynthesis, converting solar energy and carbon dioxide into food. The food energy stored in algae, microscopic phytoplankton, sea grasses, and other plants is the first link in most oceanic food chains. Animals either eat these plants or eat other animals that do. The role of aquatic plants is no less significant on land. Most of the oxygen in the atmosphere comes from them.

The king angelfish inhabits the rocky, clear waters of the Gulf of California. Like other angelfish, it is active mostly during the day. *Below:* A hogfish searches for mollusks off the Galápagos Islands. This brilliantly colored member of the wrass family is found in all tropical and temperate marine waters.

Plants are most abundant in the shallow, sun-drenched waters that rim the world's oceans. It is in these coastal areas – the beaches, bays, marshes, and swamps – where many of the oceans' young grow and develop. Nutrient-rich rivers flow into the salty bays of the sea, creating havens for maturing clams, crabs, oysters, and other shellfish. Muddy salt marshes and tangled mangrove swamps act as nurseries for the young of dozens of species of crustaceans, fishes, and insects. These areas also help sustain numerous birds – cormorants, gulls, herons, pelicans, sandpipers, and terns spend much of their lives in these shallow ocean habitats.

Thick groves of giant kelp, a kind of seaweed, grow off the coasts of China and Japan and along the west coast of the United States and Canada. While limited to cold water, this prolific plant can grow more than a foot (30 cm) a day. Gas-filled bladders on the stalk keep the plant from sinking. Kelp provides food and shelter for abalones, barnacles, eels, lobsters, mussels, octopuses, sea urchins, and snails. Fish feeding on some of these smaller creatures are, in turn, eaten by sea lions and seals.

A frightened puffer fish fills itself with water. Flat spines on its body become erect weapons when the fish is inflated. Many species of puffer fish are poisonous to predators, including people. *Right:* To keep from drifting with the currents, a seahorse curls its tail around a plant. Remaining nearly motionless, the upright fish will draw small crustaceans and other animals into its mouth.

Opposite: This green moray eel looks more ferocious than it really is. A gentle animal unless provoked, it opens its mouth to take in water for respiration. Its sharp, non-poisonous teeth hold small prey. *This page:* A lionfish slowly swims in warm coastal waters along a coral reef. Its mane-like fins, filled with venom, are used to catch and kill prey. *Below:* A snowflake moray eel peeks out of a crevice in a coral reef. The eel stays out of sight during the day. At night, it darts in and out of its hiding place looking for fish and octopuses.

In warm tropical waters off the coast of Florida, Africa, Australia, Brazil, and elsewhere, coral reefs support communities of life. Despite their plantlike appearance and stationary life-style, corals are polyps – hollow, cylindrical animals whose lower ends attach to the sea bottom, the hulls of sunken ships, or some other hard surface. Their mouth, encircled by brightly colored tentacles, filters food from the water.

The polyps secrete the stuff reefs are made of – calcium carbonate, or limestone. Depositing the limestone around themselves cements the polyps in place. Algae living on the coral provide the animal with oxygen and other nutrients it needs to produce its limestone shelter. In return, the algae get the carbon dioxide they need for photosynthesis. Within this symbiotic relationship, polyps multiply, form a colony, and eventually a reef. The animals live only on the surface of the reef; the rest of the branching complex is dead rock, the limestone remains of generations of polyps.

The giant clam of the South Pacific can grow up to 5 feet (1.5cm) in length and can weigh as much as 500 pounds (227kg). Algae living on the clam provide it with oxygen and food and turn its mantle a brilliant blue. *Below:* A newly hatched octopus swims by drawing water into its body and releasing it through an opening under its head. If an octopus loses one of its eight tentacles in a battle, it will grow another to replace it.

Hundreds of animal species live in and around coral reefs. Small striped fish seek hiding places from prowling groupers and barracudas. Colorful sponges and sea anemones attach themselves to the reef wall. Some sea urchins and worms burrow into it. Crown-of-thorns starfish feed on coral polyps, dissolving them with digestive juices flowing from their stomachs. Parrotfish feed on algae they scrape off the reef surface with their beak-shaped teeth.

About 12,000 years ago at the end of the last ice age, massive sheets of ice melted, raising sea levels and flooding coastlines worldwide. Today, that submerged land forms a shallow sea bottom that extends less than a mile in some areas to many hundreds of miles in others. Called the continental shelf, it slopes gently downward, often ending at the edge of cliffs that plunge several miles to the depths of the sea.

This colorful creature has several names—
nudibranch, sea slug, aquatic snail. Like its
relative the clam, it is a mollusk. It feeds
on sea anemones and jellyfish, incorporating
the stinging cells of these animals into its
own skins. *Right:* In the Red Sea, a nudibranch called Spanish dancer breathes
through exposed feathery gills.

Spiny lobsters line up off the shores of Cozumel. In the spring and fall, tens of thousands of these 2-foot-long (60cm) lobsters form long rows and migrate within tropical waters.

At the foot of these cliffs lie flat, featureless areas – the abyssal plains. Rising out of these broad regions is the longest mountain range on earth. The Mid-Ocean Ridge runs down the entire length of the Atlantic Ocean, curves through the Indian Ocean south of Africa and Australia, and then parallels South America in the Pacific Ocean as far as Mexico. The Azores, Easter Island, Iceland, and the Galápagos Islands are peaks that have broken the surface along this 45,000-mile (27,405km) chain.

The mountains of the ocean, like some of the mountains on land, are created by the splitting apart of the earth's crustal plates as they slip and slide on the planet's liquid core. Through the cracks, lava erupts and forms mounds, which over several million years grow into mountains. This ongoing mountain-making process, called seafloor spreading, rocks the planet with earthquakes and widens the ocean floor by about two inches (5cm) each year.

With a lung the length of its body, a sea snake can stay underwater for hours at a time. It breathes air through nostrils placed on top of its head. Its venomous fangs are used primarily for defense. *Below:* Another aquatic reptile, the green sea turtle lives in tropical waters, feeding on crustaceans, mollusks, and turtle grass.

Eagle rays gracefully glide through the water on winglike fins. Found worldwide in tropical and subtropical waters, they have spines at the base of their tail. *Below:* A stringray lies camouflaged in the sand off the coast of Ponape, an island in the North Pacific. Stingrays use their teeth to catch and crush prey, reserving their poisonous spines located under their taii for defense.

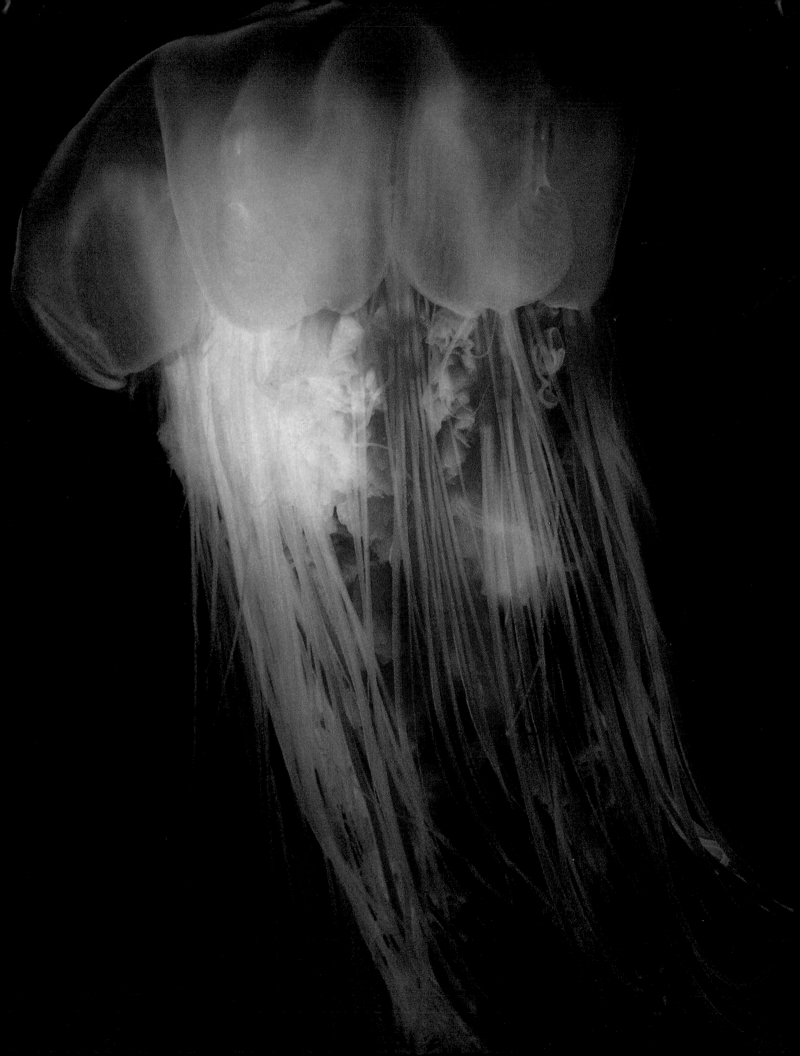

Long narrow ditches, or trenches, form where the earth's plates converge, forcing one plate beneath the other. Trenches often run adjacent to coastlines, where the dense oceanic crust sinks beneath the lighter continents. They are especially common around the periphery of the Pacific Ocean. Between Australia and Japan, the deepest place in the ocean, the Mariana Trench, extends nearly seven miles (11km) down.

It was long believed that the immense pressure, near-freezing temperatures, and total lack of sunlight in the deep sea would make life there impossible. But not so. Up through certain cracks, or rifts, in the seafloor comes not only lava, but also heated water, forming a type of spring not unlike the sulfur springs in Yellowstone National Park. Specialized bacteria, unknown until 1977, chemically interact with the elements suspended in these underwater springs. What green plants do with sunlight, the bacteria do with chemicals. Through a process called chemosynthesis, the bacteria begin a food chain that supports a host of organisms— clams, crabs, fishes, mussels, octopuses, and tube worms. In the last 13 years, scientists have discovered more than a hundred new animal species near these deep ocean springs.

Opposite: **A large arctic jellyfish moves through the water by expanding and contracting its bell-shaped body.** *This page:* **Like other types of jellyfish, this box jellyfish in the Caribbean Sea consists mostly of water. A jellylike material between two layers of cells gives the animal its buoyancy.** *Below:* **The delicate, but dangerous, tentacles of an arctic jellyfish can inject a paralyzing poison into prey.**

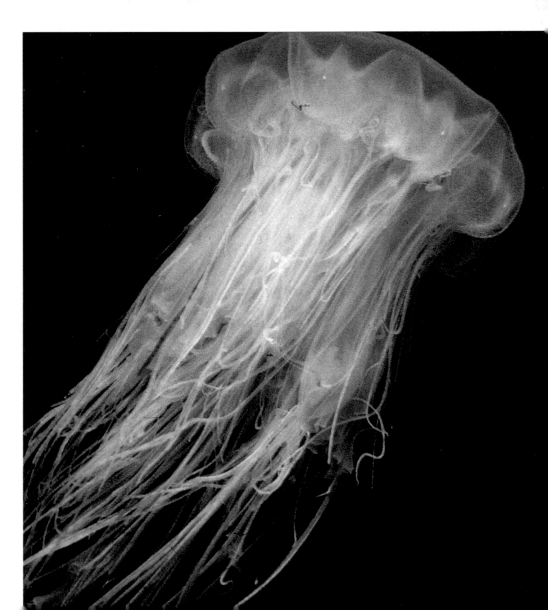

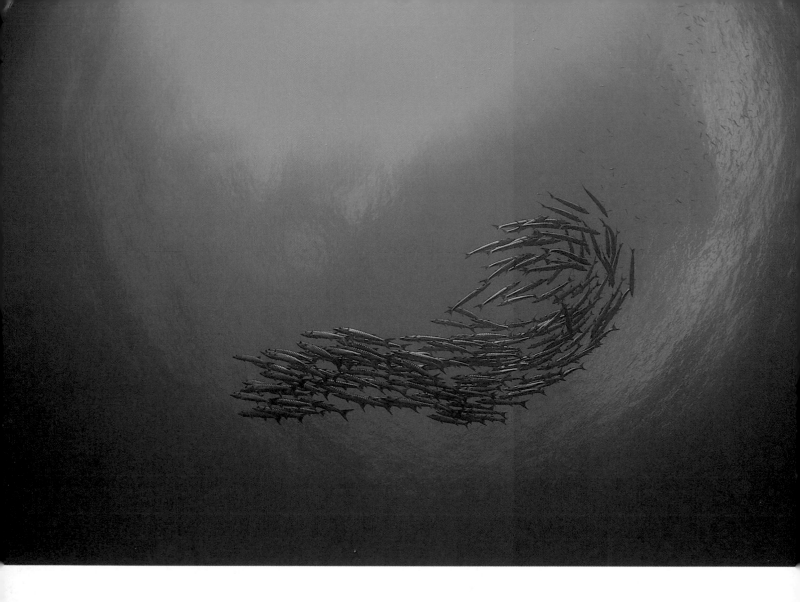

Preceding page: A school of grunts swims off the Virgin Islands. Grunts are named for the sound they make when grinding together their small, pointed teeth. *This page:* A school of barracudas prowls off the coast of Papua New Guinea. These 3-foot-long (1m) cousins of the great barracuda have long, sharp teeth and will prey on nearly any animal available. Jackfish hunt in groups for small reef fishes in the Red Sea. The school breaks up at night to rest, and then regroups the next day. *Opposite:* Red snappers and jackfish are among the various kinds of marine life found in the warm waters of the Red Sea, which is not fed by inland rivers, but by the Indian Ocean.

A leopard shark rests on the bottom of the Red Sea. Unlike most sharks, it is able to pump water through its gills to obtain oxygen. Sharks dispel water through large slits on their sides. *Below:* Grey reef sharks often gather along reefs where strong ocean currents bring a concentration of prey.

Seafloor springs are not the oceans' only source of inorganic chemicals. Rivers and rain also deposit minerals into the oceans. And within the oceans themselves, nutrients are used and reused. Both dead plants and animals, as well as animal waste, release nitrogen and other nutrients as they break down. The decomposing material sinks to the seafloor. It is the constant upwelling of this sediment that supports much of the ocean wildlife.

This is especially true around Antarctica where minerals and oxygen continually rise from the seafloor to support a complex web of life. Drifting phytoplankton start the process by converting solar energy and oxygen into food. Animals such as jellyfish, krill, and worms eat the plants. Krill, small shrimplike crustaceans, are the main food of fishes, penguins, seals, and baleen whales. A blue whale, the largest animal that has ever lived, may consume several tons of krill a day.

Of all the shark species, scalloped hammerhead sharks have one of the largest brains in relation to their body weight. Found in warm waters, these sharks often migrate in huge schools. All hammerheads have an eye and a nostril at each end of their head. *Right:* **As a hammerhead shark swims, it swings its massive head from side to side. This may enable it to see and smell over a larger area than would otherwise be possible.**

Preceding page: A great white shark has rows of pointed teeth with serrated edges. When a tooth breaks off or wears down, another one rotates forward to replace it. Fierce predators, great white sharks live in warm, shallow seas where they feed on dolphins, sea lions, seals, turtles, and other sharks. *This page:* Searching for squid, a blue shark cruises near the surface of deep water. *Below:* Aided by ocean currents, blue sharks may migrate more than 1,500 miles (2,414 km) between seasons.

Krill also live in the Arctic Ocean where seals, sharks, and whales feed on them. This northernmost ocean is more-stable – perhaps because it is surrounded by more land – than the waters around the South Pole. With fewer nutrients in circulation, there are fewer animals.

In the Atlantic Ocean, the Sargasso Sea is a gyre about two-thirds of the size of the continental United States. Rimmed in part by the Gulf Stream, this area remains calmer, saltier, and warmer than surrounding waters. Trapped in these isolated waters are clumps of yellow-brown seaweed, called sargassum. Like kelp, sargassum is buoyed by water-filled sacs and supports abundant life.

The three-inch-long (8cm) sargassum fish, sporting leaflike appendages, easily hide in the seaweed. Crabs and shrimps, in camouflaged coloring, also find refuge here. The Sargasso Sea is a nursery for developing eels, marlins, sailfish, swordfish, and tuna. Once grown, these animals take to the open sea, a domain they share with such wide-ranging predators as sharks and whales.

Opposite: Bottlenose dolphins (top) leap gracefully out of the water to breathe. At about 5 feet (2m) long, dolphins are the smallest whales. The common dolphin (bottom) may travel in herds of hundreds, or even thousands. A language of clicks, squeaks, and whistles allows them to communicate with each other. Using echolocation, they find food and avoid sharks.

Ocean animals range from microscopic zooplankton, silent drifters of the sea, to whales, mobile giants that use sound to communicate over great distances. There are spineless sponges lacking organs, muscles, and nerves as well as bony fish lined with sensory receptors. Clams, oysters, and snails, like coral, secrete their own building material to house their soft, fleshy bodies. Crabs, lobsters, and shrimps shed and replace external skeletons as they grow. These aquatic insects have compound eyes, two pairs of antennae, and segmented bodies.

Life forms in the oceans have taken on numerous, and often bizarre, adaptations. Consider some of the ways that animals of the sea feed, move, reproduce, and defend themselves. Clams, mussels, and oysters simply filter food from seawater; torpedo rays seek out and shock prey with electric organs; and swordfish use their extended snouts like machetes to kill and mangle fish. Scallops move forward by expelling jets of water from their

Opposite: **A blue whale shoots air out of its lungs through paired nostrils, or blowholes, on the top of its head. A moist spray goes up as the whale exhales. After breathing in, the whale will close its blowholes and dive.** *This page:* **A humpback whale slaps the water with its tail. Is the motion playful, or is it a message to other whales? It is known that humpbacks communicate by an eerie musical language; males seeking mates emit a rhythmic series of "yups," "chirps," "ees," and other sounds. After humpbacks breed in warm southern waters, they head north. The whales may swim close to coasts during migration. This humpback surveys its surroundings.**

Preceding page: Humpbacks breach, or hurl their bodies up and out of the water, more than any other whale species. Perhaps they do it to stun fish and other prey, to shake off lice, or to show other whales their strength. *This page:* Belugas, or white whales, spend all of their lives in cold Arctic waters. These whales are born dark, but turn white by the time they are six or seven years old. *Below:* Feeding in shallow water, a gray whale comes up with a mouthful of kelp. Seawater strained through comblike plates, called baleen, hanging from the whale's upper jaw renders a feast of small animals. Barnacles and whale lice live on the whale's skin.

A killer whale pokes its head out of the water to search for signs of prey. As many as several dozen killer whales will live together, forming a pod. Cooperative hunters, they feed on fish, squid, penguins, sea lions, seals, and even other whales. *Below:* Iridescent narwhals cluster in cold water between two ice floes. Males sport a long tooth that spirals as far as 10 feet (3m) out of their mouths. The tusk may help them attract mates.

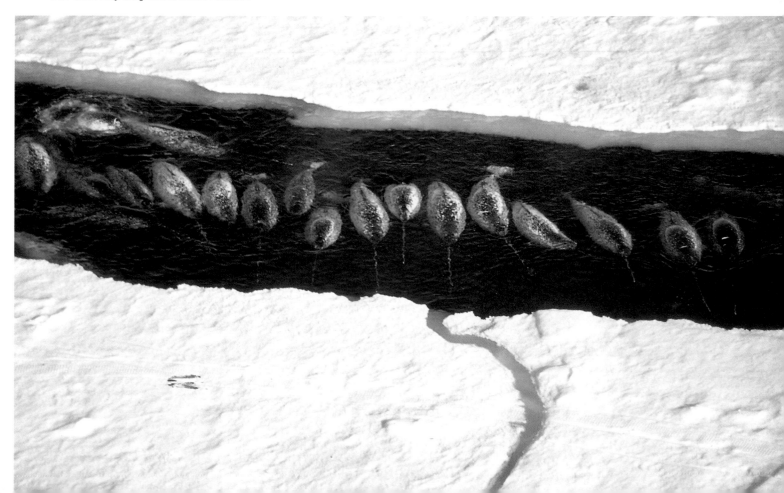

A sargassum crab blends into the seaweeds of its home in the Sargasso Sea. *Right:* A sea otter floats on its back above a kelp forest. In rich feeding grounds along the coasts of the northern Pacific, sea otters dive for clams, fish, and sea urchins. *Opposite:* The panther flounder ranges in saltwater from Africa to Australia. Like all flounders, its eyes are on the same side of its head. The fish swims on its side, moving its tail up and down as it goes.

clamping valves; barnacles, permanently fastened to rocks, piers, or other animals, never move; and tunas and sharks, lacking the gas bladder that keeps most fish afloat, will sink if they ever stop moving. To attract a mate for reproduction, damselfish make sounds, and lantern fish illuminate themselves with light-producing cells on their body. When threatened, puffer fish erect sharp spines by inflating themselves with water; garden eels hide in tunnels dug in the sandy ocean bottom; and octopuses change the color, pattern, and texture of their skin.

The most visible residents of the sea are fish. Most have scales – a kind of bony armor – that streamline and protect them. Fish also have fins, thin membranes that fan out from their body. It is their fins that enable fish to stay balanced, move forward, and turn and stop. Bat fish also use their fins to walk on the ocean floor, and flying fish glide briefly above the surface on winglike fins.

All fish breathe through gills, tiny organs laced with blood vessels that absorb oxygen from the water. Two sets of gills are located on either side of their head. Gill openings – usually a small round hole – are covered by a thin flap of bone that closes as a fish takes in water and opens as water is pushed out.

Along the sides of most fish, just under the skin, is a row of supersensitive nerves called a lateral line. By alerting fish to slight changes in water flow and pressure, lateral lines allow fish swimming in schools to rise, dive, turn, and twist as one unit. Swimming in schools – like flying in flocks – helps keep animals safe. Great numbers of anchovy, grunts, jackfish, or smelt swimming in schools often scare or confuse enemies. And while those on the fringe of the school may be taken by a predator, the group as a whole remains safe.

For centuries, people have used the oceans to travel from continent to continent. Fish and other seafoods, along with corals, pearls, and sponges, have long been harvested; the current annual yield exceeds 88

Top to bottom: An inhabitant of the Galápagos Islands, a marine iguana eats algae found on rocks both above and below the water's surface. The 2-foot-long (60cm) iguanas coexist with creatures such as sally lightfoot crabs. Each year from San Francisco to Baja California, nearly 100,000 northern elephant seals come ashore to breed. The males fiercely defend their harems and breeding spots. *Opposite:* A green sea turtle uses its hind flippers to dig a nest along the shore of a Galápagos island. The turtle will lay more than 100 eggs, cover them with sand, and return to the sea. Two months later, the newly hatched turtles will make their own way to the water. *Overleaf:* Members of the seal family, California sea lions breed along the California coast and in the Galápagos Islands.

million (80 million metric) tons. And our high-tech probing of the oceans has increased our use of ocean resources. Today, giant kelp, harvested off the coasts of California and China, is used as an additive in foods, medicines, and cosmetics. We extract bromine, magnesium, and salt from the sea, and in time, the fist-size lumps of copper, iron, and manganese that now cover wide areas of the ocean floor will be plucked.

Efforts are already underway to turn the raw power of the oceans into usable energy. The action of tides currently generates electricity in Canada, China, France, and the Soviet Union, and similar plants are being considered for the coasts of Alaska and Maine. In Norway, a prototype plant converts wave motion into electricity. Power plants operating in Japan and Hawaii exploit the solar energy stored in ocean waters. And a type of underwater windmill, designed by engineers in the United States, may someday harness the power of the Gulf Stream and other currents.

Opposite: An intruder annoys a male, or bull, California sea lion. As many as 40 females, or cows, may belong to his harem. The bull mates with all of them, and in the following spring, each cow will bear a single pup. *This page:* At a sea lion rookery, bulls bellow and bark. Acute hearing allows female sea lions to recognize the sound of their own pups in the crowd. Sea lions feed on fish and squid and, in turn, are preyed upon by sharks and killer whales.

Fish attract a bevy of birds off the coast of California. Brown pelicans, Brandt's cormorants, and Heermann's gulls all have a hook-tipped bill, which helps them grasp fish. Pelicans also use their huge throat pouch to scoop up fish. *Below:* Immature brown pelicans, browner overall than the adults, begin feeding themselves after they fledge, at about 12 weeks of age. *Opposite:* Northern gannets soar on long, tapered wings above cold North Atlantic waters. From great heights, these birds will dive headlong into the water after fish, folding their wings just before impact.

Thousands of northern gannets nest on the rocky cliffs of Cape St. Mary's along the coast of Newfoundland. Gannets spend about half of the year incubating eggs and raising young on land, and the other half of the year at sea.

This page: Like northern gannets, wandering albatrosses only come ashore to breed. Courting albatrosses tap their bills together. Black-browed albatrosses (*center*) also nest in large colonies. Pairs gather on remote subantarctic islands, where the female lays a single egg. These large seabirds mate for life. Pointed bill and wings distinguish this common tern (*bottom*) from its gull relatives. Common terns nest in colonies on inland shores as well as on sandy beaches of the Atlantic and Pacific oceans.

By natural design, almost all of the fresh water that falls on land originates in the sea. Once water evaporates from the oceans, it forms clouds, and then falls as rain and snow. Because water temperatures change more slowly than air temperatures, the oceans moderate earth's climate, keeping the planet from dangerous extremes of hot and cold. That the oceans and the air are linked is certain, but scientists are just now beginning to understand the depth of this connection and the extent to which the oceans affect our lives.

That is why our treatment of the oceans is a growing concern. The U.S. alone pumps about 32 billion gallons (121 billion liters) of toxic chemicals and sewage into the sea every day. In the Atlantic Ocean off the U.S. coast, sludge from urban waste treatment plants lies dozens of feet deep. Mineral-rich sediment, the lifeblood of the oceans, lies buried underneath.

Opposite: Alaska's coast provides perfect nesting sites for these horned puffins. Adults can carry three or four small fish at a time in their bill. *This page:* Atlantic puffins gather along the coast of Newfoundland. Chicks from this colony may be moved to islands off Maine in an effort to repopulate that area. *Right:* Tufted puffins breed along the West Coast from Alaska to California. As with other puffins, their bills will turn dull after the breeding season. All puffins spend winters far out to sea.

Fertilizers and phosphates dumped into rivers end up in the oceans where they cause unsightly and deadly explosions of algae growth. The algae smother marine life by depriving the water of oxygen. Tons of dead clams and mussels have washed ashore the Adriatic Sea, now largely coated with green slime after years of receiving polluted waters from Italy's Po River.

Offshore oil drilling takes place in increasingly fragile areas despite accidents that have blackened beaches and killed marine animals. The death toll from the Alaskan oil spill in the spring of 1989 stands at 1,000 sea otters, 148 eagles, and 34,000 other birds. And U.S. government biologists have said that these figures could represent only 10 to 30 percent of the final total.

At the same time that we are exposing the ocean environment to poisons, we are exhausting animal populations by fishing. In recent years, overfishing has led to reduced catches of cod, haddock, pollack, redfish, and hack off New England. Fish used primarily for feed stocks, such as herring in Europe and anchovy in Peru, are seriously depleted. Spiny lobsters and queen conch in the Caribbean; abalone, Dungeness crab, and king crab in the Pacific; and bluefin tuna in the Atlantic and the Mediterranean are all in serious trouble. Salmon have been nearly wiped out in the Atlantic.

Opposite: Huddled on an island beach off the coast of Alaska, walruses doze in the sun. After resting on shore, they will hunt for food – clams, crabs, snails, and shrimps.
This page: Both male and female walruses have long ivory tusks. Poking these teeth on ice, the animals raise their bulky bodies out of the water. Males also use the teeth to joust with one another. Their tough hides prevent most injuries.

A leopard seal rests between meals. At home in southern waters, leopard seals feed on krill, penguins, seabirds, and squid. Harp seals, at the other end of the earth, prefer small crustaceans. The pup's white fur will soon be replaced by a coat like its mother's.

A polar bear waking from a nap is hard to see against the snowy terrain of its Arctic home. A polar bear's dense fur and thick layer of fat protect it from the cold. Nearly grown bears playfully wrestle with one another. Cubs, born in dens under snowbanks, may stay with their mother for more than two years.

Preceding page: Agile on land, polar bears can reach speeds up to 35 miles (56.3 km) an hour. In the water, these slow but powerful swimmers prey mainly on seals. *This page:* Emperor penguins waddle across the ice of Antarctica. Although they cannot fly, they are excellent swimmers. The largest of the penguins, emperors stand about 4 feet (1.2m) high.

Top to bottom: Adélie penguins spend the Antarctic winters at sea, returning each year to their rocky ancestral breeding grounds. Chinstrap penguins may chase a pair of Adélies from their nest site and claim it for their own. Gentoos, with flipperlike wings and webbed feet, dive into the water in search of fish and krill. *Overleaf:* King penguins stand beak-to-beak on their rookery. Parents take turns incubating their single egg on the tops of their feet; warm folds of belly keep the egg warm.

Fishing doesn't just kill fish. Thousands of miles of abandoned fishing nets trap and kill countless sea turtles, seabirds, seals, and whales each year. Many countries, including Mexico, Spain, the U.S., and Venezuela, engage in a method of tuna fishing that needlessly kills herds of dolphins. Schools of tuna often swim beneath dolphins, and large circular nets used to catch the tuna also trap and suffocate the air-breathing dolphins.

The oceans are not the empty silent places they were once thought to be. Nor are they the dreaded domain of sea monsters and ship-swallowing whirlpools. These old myths are gone. But new ones have taken their place. That what we dump in the oceans is gone forever. That the oceans are somehow self-cleaning and impervious to harm. These myths continue to be shattered as undersea exploration uncovers more truths about the oceans and their strange and beautiful inhabitants.

Index of Photography